Looking at Birds and Other Wild Life

Looking at Birds and Other Wild Life

Nell Hutchison

VANTAGE PRESS
New York

FIRST EDITION

Copyright © 1998 by Nell Hutchison

Published by Vantage Press, Inc.
516 West 34th Street, New York, New York 10001

Manufactured in the United States of America
ISBN: 0-533-12600- 2

0 9 8 7 6 5 4 3 2 1

To the birds who write their own poetry
in motion and patterns

Contents

Foreword

In this collection, Nell Hutchison has captured the elusive spirit of birds in a stunning series of poems. Although other wildlife is occasionally featured, this book is primarily about birds: marsh birds, blackbirds, city crows, redwings, flickers, and ducks. These bright, swift, singing, and swimming birds will fly through your imagination long after you have put aside this book. Concise and imagistic, these poems are haiku-like in their observational precision and impact. Nell Hutchison is a fine lyric poet and in her skilled hands, each of these poems is quick and bright, refracting like a crystal. To read this collection is to enter a world of mist, birdsong and light, a world of flashing primary colors—the lyrical world of Nell Hutchison's birds.

—Carol Frith

(Carol Frith is co-editor of *EKPHRASIS*, a literary journal, and was the first place winner of the 1997 Blue Unicorn open poetry competition as well as a runner-up in the 1997 Howard Nemerov Sonnet competition.)

*Looking at Birds and
Other Wild Life*

Quail

Nine top knots
weave through dry grass
fabric of a family

Mist of birds
settles on marsh
tranquillity

Triple strand of black birds
looped over street
S C A T T E R
like ebony beads

In the midst of the storm
one thousand raindrops
cling trembling yet
tenaciously to the
oak's bare
branches

City Crows

In somber garb
with hoarse lament
they come
like mourners
to a wake

White blossoms
swirl on black pavement
Fragrant snow mocks
winter

Sunday Morning
in Yoncalla

Pears hang heavy
on limber branches
Pale peach glads
lean lazily
on picket fence
Cock crows once
Gray-striped cat
yawns
goes back to sleep
Buzzing fly
magnifies silence

Young Camellia

Crimson petals drench ground
I watch them fall and wonder
where the years have gone

Swarm of birds
clinging
to top
of barren tree
flutter
to ground
like autumn leaves

Bird Fire

The marsh explodes
billowing black
streak of gold
crimson flash
a moment
so intense
it consumes
itself and I
am left alone
in the sanctuary
holding the ash
of memory
and one
black feather.

Crows
return to trees
at dusk

Where
have they been
all day?

Butterfly with folded wings
contemplates
length and breadth
of blossom

Above the Fog

Grazing cows
pepper verdant hills
Native oaks stretch out
aged arms
Water pools in hollows
Blue sky arcs
in ecstasy

Four red-crested
speckled-chested flickers
perched on power line
listen with
heads-up attention
while house finch
trills
his morning
song

Ducks

Sparrows flit from limb to limb
Pigeons tumble playfully
tossed by the wind
but ducks
fly with a purpose
straight on
as if they know
exactly
where they are going

Winter Patterns

Miniature webs carpet
dew-drenched lawn
each gauzy strand
anchored
to a blade of grass

above the lawn
trees reach out lacy arms
in silhouetted silence
to welcome
the rising sun

Distance Stills the Water

River
satin ribbon tying
loose ends of velvet hills
and checkered woolen valleys
into patterned
tapestry

Rapids
white tulle
cascading
into oblivion

Mist
shimmering silk
diaphanous
floating free

In the Slow Lane

The radio plays
"Sweet Darlin' "
"Kalamity"
lies at my feet
I yawn
then fall asleep

Chipmunk

at roadside
salutes
passing cars
then races
across road
tail at attention

Underside of
butterfly wings
translucent
pattern
on delicate
fabric

The delta breeze
shakes
the camphor tree
into a rush
of whispering

Humming Bird Dog Fight

Staccato tones strafe air
Iridescent fighters
needle nose to tail
dive through oak
and then with
chandelle maneuver
zoom up and out
of sight

Raven

strides down road
as if
he owns it

Snail hitches ride
on power mower
to seek new horizons

Surprise

Ruby-throated bud
perched
on tip of rose stem
suddenly takes flight

Keening swallows
return return and return
to destroyed nests
in motel eaves
then catching on in unison
they wheel in mid-flight
and are gone

Mockingbird on tail
of crow
Crow too slow

Mockingbird
flies straight at
chain-link fence and
lands in diamond—
head
in one yard
tail
in another

Pigeons in flight

SHIFT

FORMATION

like an Escher drawing

A flock of birds

    fling   themselves

                          across the sky

like

    autumn

      leaves

        caught

          up

  in a windstorm

Magnetic Moment

Robins, sparrows, jays
and mockingbirds
are pulled
in swift succession
from bare-limbed trees
into green-leafed
black-berried branches
until the small tree
quivers in excitement.

Then one by one
they break
away.

The tree
stands quiet.

Sea Gull

wings at full sail
tacks
into wind

Raven rides
crest of tallest pine
leaning into wind
surfer hanging ten

Traffic

It is a   blustery
    day   everything
       in   motion
Dark clouds   scurry
    across   gray sky
Birds   wing   here
    and   there   with   no
    apparent   destination
    and   pedestrians   seem   in a big
    hurry   to   get   who   knows   where

While   I   encased
in   my   car
wait   calmly
for   a   green light

Freeze Frame

woman pauses
hand extended
with quarter held
between thumb and finger

Tiny black-yellow beetle
rests on parking meter knob

Hand moves
quarter drops in place
Knob turns
beetle spreads
his wings and flies

Kalamity

sleeps in out basket.
Writer must overcome
many obstacles.

Dove and Mockingbird
at opposite ends
of TV antenna
nature in balance

Crow Feather

Holding	it
turning	it in my hand
I count	thirteen
beads	of moisture
clinging	to the concave
side	clustered diamonds
in an	ebony setting
I carry	it
lightly	shielded from
the sun	but when
my walk	ends
only	one droplet
still	sparkles
a	solitaire

At dusk
ten white doves
rise and circle twice
a benediction

Painted Desert

Restless wind
capricious artist
never finishes
his masterpiece

High Wire Act

Twelve blackbirds
swing gently to and fro
on three parallel power lines

Scolding blue jay
swoops
Silver tabby
ducks

Two ducks race
        neck and neck
            across twilit sky
            to invisible
                finish line

            Ink bottle
            lies on side
        blue kitten tracks
        lead to culprit

Wildlife

White wings tipped
with black, whooping cranes,
mother, father and
adolescent son, soar
across continent
to breeding grounds
in northern Canada. While

at wildlife sanctuary,
after futile attempt
to extract semen
from recalcitrant male,
a biologist mutters,
"It's not easy
to breed captive
whooping cranes."

Inland Gulls

swarm over garbage mountain
ah, what vistas sacrificed
for
satiety